CONTENTS

© Edition, photographs and text:
Charles Blanc-Pattin (Editions Photoguy), Editions Molipor and Editorial Escudo de Oro, S.A.

Distribution in Monaco
© **EDITIONS MOLIPOR** 8 rue de Lorete 98000 MONACO. Tel (377) 93 50 72 37

Distribution in France
© **EDITIONS PHOTOGUY** 06330 ROQUEFORT-LES-PINS. Tel 04 93 77 17 28

INTRODUCTION

Ideally located between the Sea and the Mountains, the French Riviera stretches from the Italian border to the Western limit of the *Département* (administrative district) of Var.

The evocative French term for the Riviera: «la Côte d'Azur», literally the Azure Coast, was coined more than a century ago by the poet Stephen Liegeard. However, it is a blanket term that cloaks the astounding variety, characteristic of this part of France.

The historical variety of the area allows the traveller to journey from prehistoric sites to medieval castles, from Roman ruins to hilltop perched villages, from Romanesque churches to more recent works.

Its geographical variety offers sumptuous landscapes from the jagged, multicoloured rocks of l'Estérel through long, apparently languorous bays, past sheer cliffs that give way to the cornices of Eze, Menton or Monaco, up through the countless, steep-sided valleys of the Nice hinterland.

Environmental variety takes in large, busy, commercial towns, along with well-preserved villages that have witnessed an intense and rich history; it goes from the jovial, bustling, crowded market of Cours Saleya to the huge open spaces of the Mercantour Park, a paradise for chamois, marmots and nature lovers.

Its varied climate allows visitors to dangle their feet in the deep blue sea, while contemplating, in the distance, the snow capped summits of the winter sport resorts of Auron, Isola 2000 or Valberg.

The variety of vegetation combines the scents of aromatic herbs and the perfume of mimosa, rose, jasmine or lavender with that of the astonishing species collected together in exotic botanical gardens.

Nor must we forget to mention the softly swaying palms; the parasol pines, fiercely clinging to the rocks; the hustle and bustle of the towns, the quiet of the villages; or the smooth cascade of streams over solid rocks. All of this bathed in the myriad golden rays of a generous sun streaming out of a bright blue cloudless sky. All of this combining with the flavours of an enviable cuisine based on thyme, olive oil, garlic and basil.

What a marvellous alchemy is encapsulated on the Riviera!

▲ *An Orange Tree from the Menton district.*

Boats in the port. ▶

▼ *The Basilica of Saint Michael the Archangel.*

MENTON

Menton is a border town to the east of the Maritime-Alps, the final stop before entering Italy. Well protected from the northern winds, this village is the warmest resort on the Riviera, which makes it a magnet for retired people. Its mild climate is particularly suited to orange, mandarin and lemon trees and citrus groves are omnipresent in the terrain surrounding the village.

The first historical mention of Menton is from the 13th century, when *Charles the first of Anjou* passed through it. In 1456, *Lambert Grimaldi*, the Lord of Menton, was named as successor to the Prince of Monaco, but soon after had to put down, with the aid of the *Duke of Milan*, a revolt of his own subjects. Menton was linked to Monaco until 1848 and later opted to become part of France in 1860.

The most important building in Menton is the **Basilique de Saint-Michel Archange** constructed in the 17th century. In the heart of the church can be found a 16th century altarpiece by *André Manchello* and numerous objects of art, such as an 18th century statue of Saint Michel in polychrome wood. Worthy of mention too is the **Chapelle des Pénitents Blancs** and the **Hôtel de Ville** (town hall) whose wedding salon was decorated by the painter, poet and dramatist *Jean Cocteau*.

The **Musée Municipal** is also very interesting. The ground floor is dedicated to archaeological finds, which include the skull of a Cro-Magnon Man, while the first floor has an important collection of paintings.

The **Musée Jean Cocteau** with a fine collection of tapestries, drawings, watercolours and oil paintings of great value, can be found in a 16th century fortress.

Another interesting site is the **Jardin Botanic et Exotique** (Botanical Gardens) in which there is a profusion of all sorts of Mediterranean plants.

General view of Menton. ▼

▲ *The Basilica of Saint Michael the Archangel: The Choir stalls and the Archangel in gold leaf on wood.*

▼ *View of the Port.*

Aerial View. ▲

During the **Carnival** period, Menton becomes the centre of a series of over the top activities attracting numerous tourists, particularly while the **Citrus fair** is on. During this fete, in the gardens of the Biovés, there is a magnificent exhibition using only citrus fruits for decoration. Participants are given a theme and then try to outdo each other in originality and artistry. On the **Sea Front**, parades are organised using floats decorated solely with lemons and oranges. It is a spectacle that is full of life, colour and light, especially striking for the incredible contrast between the blue sky and the yellow and orange of the citrus fruits.

Citrus Festival: a float and ▶
the citrus fruit exhibition.

The Mentonnais Region

STE-AGNES

This curious medieval town clings to the foot of an impressive chalk cliff. Its enclosed houses merging with the adjacent Chapel of **St Sebastian** and the ruins of its castle. Site of an ancient Roman fort, the castle was repaired after Saracen raids in the 9th and 10th centuries. It was then sold to the *Grimaldi* family from Monaco in the 16th century. The village allied with its neighbour Sospel and rebelled, remaining a free commune until 1789 when it became French. The highest point on the castle is some 800 metres high and from this vantage point the panorama is magnificent. There is a superb view over Menton, the Mediterranean, Italy, and the Bay of Garavan, sometimes even out to Corsica. At 700 metres high, yet only three kilometres from the sea, Ste-Agnès is proud of being the highest coastal village in Europe.

▲ *Saint Agnes.*

GORBIO

Set on a 370 metre high hill covered with olive groves, this charming village in the Menton region marks the confluence of the streams of Rank and Gorbio. From its rich and bygone history this medieval town, built as a citadel, has managed to preserve its winding streets, its ancient Malaussene Fountain, its cobble-stoned alleys and its archaic, wrought iron, window bars, along with its rich private residences.

▼ *The old bridge at Sospel.*

Gorbio. ▲

▲ *Castellar.*

CASTELLAR

Perched on a 365-metre knoll dominating two valleys, this ancient village, huddled among olive trees, offers the visitor a splendid panorama of the Gulf of Menton. From its affluent and distant past, this charming village has succeeded in preserving numerous witnesses of its greater days. There are the ruins of a Palace of the Lascaris, including the Lascaris Gate and the Fortified Gate, as well as an 18th century church. Castellar is also well served by numerous footpaths that offer a range of excursions to walkers of all levels.

SOSPEL

Within a circle of mountains whose slopes are covered in olive trees and vines, this cool alpine resort, 350 metres up, spreads its houses along the fringes of the *Bévéra*. The town's superb 17th century Cathedral towers above the colourful cobbles of the *Place Saint Michel*.

This charming town, in the outer Menton region, forms the centre of a circuit that includes the mountains known as the Cols de Braus, de Brouis and de Castillon. With the winter sports resorts of l'Authion nearby and its own picturesque charm, this region attracts tourists all year round.

ROQUEBRUNE CAP-MARTIN

Forming part of a large communal ensemble that extends from Menton to Monte Carlo, Roquebrune Cap-Martin is dominated by its ancient village perched 250 metres up, overlooking the sea. The Castle, four square upon its dungeon, is a real curiosity: it is in fact, the sole example of a Carolingian Castle in France. A ramble through the old town, down its steeply inclined, winding streets and stairways and past its partly covered sloping passageways, would surely be enough to convince the visitor of the rich historical heritage of Roquebrune. These elements of the town simply preserve their authenticity. Carved out of the rock, the *Rue Moncollet*, with its medieval residences, illustrates on its own the picturesque nature of the town.

▼ *Cap Martin Point.*

Old Roquebrune. ▲
Aerial view of Roquebrune-Cap-Martin. ▼

▲ *General view of the Principality.*

Located on a rocky promontory over-looking the sea, the Principality of Monaco, famous for its casino and its riches, is a tourist centre of the first order. This tiny country owes much of its popularity to its current sovereign *HRH Prince Rainier* and his late wife *HRH Princess Grace,* desgraciadamente ya fallecida.

The name of the state appears to derive from the Roman *Portus Monoeci,* the ancient port of Hercules, spoken of in many a Mediterranean legend.

Monaco, with its tranquil port and almost constant sunshine is a bene-volent oasis. It is like a white sea bird flying between the sea and the sky.

Monaco is a sizeable city, the capital of

◄ *Le Rocher (the rock).*

The throne room. ▲
The Honour Court. ▼

▲ The Prince's Palace.

The Prince's Guard. ▶

▲ *The Cathedral.*

a dream realm. The Principality comprises: Monaco, the old town, the Condamine, the port area, the new town and Monte Carlo, the rock upon which can be found the Casino and many luxury hotels.

The remains still preserved in the surrounding area bear testament to Monaco's history. There is the cave of the skeletons, where the bones of the first inhabitants of the Mediterranean were found. Around the hills can be discovered the vestiges of the massive wall which once enclosed the old city, turn-

ing it into an impregnable fortress and adding further to the port's tranquillity. It was a place where, according to Virgil and Lucain: «*neither the Eurus, nor the Zephyrs could enter*». In 43 BC, Julius Caesar concentrated his army in the port of Monaco, while he awaited the arrival of Pompey, who had taken refuge in Illyria. In the 12th century, *Frederic Redbeard*, the Emperor of Germany, gave Genoa sovereignty over Monaco and the entire Ligurian coast. It was at this time that a great Ligurian family, *the Grimaldis*, began to play a leading role

in the history of Genoa. The Grimaldi were Guelphs who went into exile when the Ghibbellins seized power in 1295. François Grimaldi became the master of the Rock of Monaco after entering the fortress disguised as a monk. From that moment on, the power of the Grimaldis over Monaco would be consolidated. France then annexed Monaco in 1509, but the Grimaldis regained autonomy for their tiny state thanks to the treaties of Burgos and Tordesillas (1512-24). The lord of Monaco then was *Augustin Grimaldi*, the bishop of Grasse, protect-

The Oceanographic Museum.

ed by *Charles the Fifth*. In 1529 the Emperor stayed at the castle for three days.

Later the Princes of Monaco enjoyed the protection of France, but during the French Revolution, Prince *Honoré the Third* was dethroned and would later die in Paris in exile.

After the treaty of Vienna, Monaco was placed under the protection of Sardinia and remained an Italian protectorate until 1860, when it once again came under the guardianship of France. The Principality enjoyed an epoch of splendour under *Charles Grimaldi III* who dedicated his life to the reconstruction of his country. His son *Albert the First* consolidated this reconstruction and established amicable relations with France.

It was during this era that Monaco began to acquire fame as a cultural cen-

Monaco

tre and a tourist resort; a fame which has not stopped growing during the reign of its current monarch HRH Prince Rainier the Third.

Among the historical monuments of Monaco, pride of place must go to the **Grimaldi Palace**, symbol of the histori-cal continuity of the Principality. Its halls make up an interesting museum with tableaux by Giorgione, Holbein, Van Loo, Champaigne, Rigaud and other artists. There is also Japanese furniture, Venetian antiques, a fresco portraying «Renown leading the Army of the Grimaldi» and the bed wherein the Duke of York died at the end of the 18th cen-tury. It is also remarkable for the Palace Archives and the Napoleonic Museum with a collection of coins stamped in Monaco and other souvenirs of the Napoleonic era.

▼ *Monte Carlo.*

The Casino. ▶

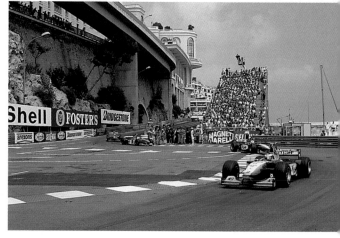

▲ *The Botanical Gardens.*

The Cathedral is the most important Monegasque architectural feature. Erected at one end of the town, it was built between 1875 and 1884 under the direction of the architect Lenormand.
Also worthy of mention are the **Musée d'Anthropologie**, the **Musée National**, the **Musée de Cires** (Wax Museum), the **Centre de Acclimatation Zoologique**, the **Musée Océanographique**, and the **Casino de Monte Carlo**. The Casino is an exquisite example of the «Liberty» style, while its halls are decorated in a baroque style.

▲ *The Augustan Trophy at La Turbie.*

LA TURBIE

Built on a ridge, the village overlooks the Principality of Monaco and its rocky coastline. Indeed, looking towards Italy, l'Estérel and Les Maures one can contemplate one of the most beautiful views on the Riviera.

La Turbie owes its fame to the celebrated **«Trophée d'Auguste»** the Augustan, or «Alpine Trophy» which the Romans erected here on the highest point of the Via Julia to honour Caesar's nephew *Augustus Octavius* and to celebrate his conquests in the Alpine region.

▲ *The Sanctuary of Our Lady of Laghet.*

LAGHET

A charming, sinuous route, which passe through the azure hills, conducts the traveller, midst the olive trees, to the village c Laghet. The **Sanctuaire de la Madone** founded in 1656, is the most celebrate site for pilgrims in the County of Nice The Cloister and the Church are covered as if by a tapestry, in countless ex-votiv offerings gathered there over the cen turies and remarkable for their naivety. I the depths of its cool green valley, Laghe offers a haven of peace in which to ex perience the serenity of its sites.

PEILLE

Founded by the Ligurians and taken b the Emperor Augustus, this picturesque historic town has hardly changed sinc the Middle Ages. Peille held a council i the 12th century and ceded its rights t the Rock of Monaco on the 11th of Ma 1179. The 17th century Church, th *Palais du Juge Mage* (Palace of th Wise Judge) and the gothic fountain ar a few of the witnesses that have sur vived to tell of the past of one of th most curious villages of the Maritim Alps area.

◀ *An old drinking fountain in Peille.*

CAP D'AIL

A commune created in 1908, the Baron le Pauville had previously launched Cap d'Ail as a Spa town in 1879. Terraced upon the lower slopes of the «Tête de Chien» (Dog's Head Mountain) the commune extends down to the edge of Monaco where a footpath, along the coast, can be followed into Monaco itself. A renowned tourist resort, Cap d'Ail is surrounded by well preserved countryside –fissures, cliffs, and footpaths– bathed in exultant fragrances from hundreds of pines, eucalyptus, rock-roses and sycamores.

Of particular note is the open-air *Jean Cocteau* Theatre, decorated with three fine mosaics by the artist.

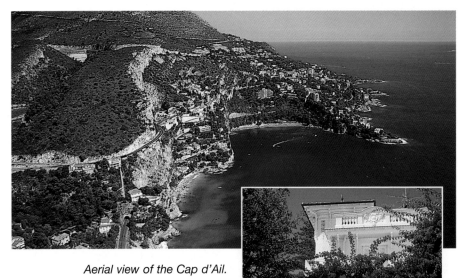

Aerial view of the Cap d'Ail.

EZE-VILLAGE

Some historians have claimed that the name of this village is derived from the Egyptian Goddess *Isis*, while others have insisted it comes from the term *visia* or *Avisiam*, which the Romans gave to look out posts on high vantage points.

Perched upon a rock, 427 metres above the sea, this town, fortified by Caesar, is a veritable eagle's nest. This ancient agricultural village, which at the beginning of the 14th century was a Guelph stronghold, saw its castle dismantled in 1706 under the orders of Louis XIV. Narrow, sloping streets, giving the village a picturesque air, lead the visitor down to the **Chapelle des Pénitents Blancs** and to the **Eglise** (Church) which is well worth looking around.

◀ *The streets of the old town.*

▼ *Aerial view over Eze and the Cap-Ferrat.*

A picturesque street in Eze-Village. ▶

The small square at the entrance to the town. ▼

From Monaco to Nice

▲ *The roofs of Eze from the Botanical Gardens.*

The **Jardin Exotique** offers an enormous variety of plants and cacti that would no doubt captivate any visitor. A charming path, fringed with pines and olive trees takes the walker towards the lower Cornice at the seashore.

▲ *The Botanical Gardens.*

Eze-sur-Mer. ▶

Aerial View. ▲

The church of Beaulieu. ▲

The Kérylos Villa. ▼

BEAULIEU

On the other side of Cap Ferrat, Beaulieu-sur-Mer is spread over an amphitheatre of hills that protect it from the winds and make it one of the warmest places on the Riviera, particularly appreciated in Winter. Villas and Luxury Hotels are scattered throughout sumptuous gardens along the sea front and along boulevards that climb the heights into the district known as *Petite Afrique* jammed in between the rocks of *Saint-Michel* and the sea. On the tip of the *Baie des Fourmis* (Ants' bay) there is the **Vila Kerylos** constructed in 1902 by the architect *Emmanual Pontremoli* for Baron *Théodore Reinach* who was a fervent Hellenist. It is a faithful reproduction of a Greek residence at the time of Pericles. Built using the finest materials, the building itself is worthy of admiration, as is the collection of antiques to be found there.

▲ *St-Jean Cap-Ferrat: La Paloma beach.*

◀ *Cap-Ferrat Point.*

The port of St-Jean. ▼

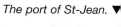

ST-JEAN CAP-FERRAT

This is a peninsula covered with pines and olive trees on which luxurious residences and properties, such as that belonging to Leopold II of Belgium, have been erected.

The **Palais Rose** (Pink Palace), constructed between 1909 and 1912 in an Italian style, was bequeathed to *L'Institut de France pour l'Academie de Beaux-Arts* by the Baroness *Ephrussi de Rotschild* in 1934. Here to be admired is a marvellous collection of art from the 16th to the 19th century; a collection of porcelain from Sèvres; of royal tapestries from Savonnerie and of 18th century furniture, some of which belonged to Marie Antoinette. The gardens surrounding the villa-museum are in every way remarkable and on summer evenings become the scene for numerous theatrical events, concerts or conferences. The principal garden is in the French style the others are in a variety of styles.

General view of St-Jean Cap-Ferrat.

The St-Hospice Chapel. ▶

▲ *La Rue Obscure (dark street).*

The port area of Villefranche.

◀ *An alleyway in old Villefranche.*

The Coubet Quay.

General view from the mid-cornice. ▲

VILLEFRANCHE-SUR-MER

Six kilometres from Nice, Villefranche-sur-Mer is one of the most well protected and picturesque ports on the Riviera. The town has maintained an air of authenticity with its multicoloured houses, typical of the area, clinging to the flanks of the mountain; its stepped passageways, its tortuous streets descending to the sea, or its winding *Rue Obscure* (dark street) close to the port.

Of equal note is the **Citadel** and **Saint Peter's Chapel**, decorated by Jean Cocteau and well worth a detour.

View of the port. ▶

▲ *The United States Quay after the climb to the Castle.*

The uncontested capital of the French Riviera, **«Nice la Belle»** has been a prized site since prehistoric times. As can be witnessed by the objects discovered in the Grimaldi caves, which attest to Man's presence there in Palaeolithic and Neolithic times.

When Avignon became the spiritual centre of the occident in the 14th century, the whole province experienced a period of literary and artistic develop-ment. While the rest of the province became definitively French, the fate of Nice became linked to the Dukes of Savoy and took a different route. Napoleon annexed Nice to France in 1793 and began his Italian campaign from there in 1796. Nice was again attached to the house of Savoy from 1814 to 1860, the year in which it became definitively French through a popular referendum.

▲ *A façade from Old Nice.*

The flower market at Cours Saleya. ▶

From the middle of the 19th century its appeal as a tourist attraction has constantly grown, in particular to rich English people who, thanks to its beauty and the mildness of its climate, have made it their favourite holiday resort.

▼ *The Cascade of the Castle.*

The beaches. ▲

The port and the Promenade des Anglais from the lower cornice. ▼

Nice

▲ The port.

The light and colour of the area around Nice have inspired countless world famous artists. The painters –*Ingres, Corot, Delacroix, Soutine, Monet, Renoir, Matisse, Picasso, Dufy, Léger. Toulouse Lautrec, Marc Chagall, Degas, Bonnard, Utrillo*– and the writers –*Balzac, Flaubert, Maupassant, Mérimée, Alexander Dumas, Montaigne, Baudelaire, Verlaine, Tolstoy, the Goncourt Brothers, Colette, Paul Valery, Maeterlink, Maugham...*– all spent time in Nice, or even took up permanent residence there. The mere presence of these artists has favoured the creation of numerous galleries and museums and given Nice a cultural and artistic vocation; without forgetting that an ample number of figures from the world of politics, sciences and finances have achieved much within the walls of the city. Nice has always welcomed celebrities, and it has cradled a few of its own illustrious sons and daughters, among whom we can mention the painters *Van Loo* and *Brea;* the astronomers *Cassini, Maraldi* and *Lascaris,* the historian *Gioffredo,* the abbot of St-Pons, *J-M de Gubernatis* «the presumed builder» of the Arènes Villa at Cimiez, *Marc de Nice* missionary to Peru and Mexico, the naturalists *Barla* and *Risso* and the generals *Masséna, Rusca* and *Garibaldi.*

However, to draw up an exhaustive list

◀ A façade from Old Nice.

The roofs from the Castle. ▼

▲ The pedestrian area of the rue Masséna.

Aerial view of the Promenade des ▲
Anglais.

of everyone who has seen Nice is, of course, impossible. Each district of the city has its own personality and jealously guards its own sense of authenticity, its architectural riches and its customs. However, one experience that must not be missed is a stroll along the **Promenade des Anglais**, which so often symbolises the capital of the Riviera, stretches languorously, along the entire length of the sea front of the Angel Bay under the discreet gaze of its grand hotels; witnesses to the city's sumptuous past. The **Négresco**, built in 1912 in the Belle Epoque architectural style, is superb, as are the **Westminster** and the **Royal**. If we add to this congregation of buildings the palms, the intense blue of the sky and the constantly changing reflections coming off the sea, a dream is seen to come true.

The Negresco Hotel. ▶

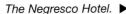

▲ *The Cours Saleya.*

One of the best ways to appreciate the attractions of Nice is to view it from the top of its castle. The panorama is unique, taking in the Angel Bay, the city itself and its surroundings. To the East, can be seen **Mont Boron** and the Port district constructed during the reign of Charles Emmanuel the Third of Savoy. To the West, the new town can be seen climbing the nearby hills. The airport can be made out in the distance and the Cap d'Antibes forms a perfect backdrop to the scene. The castle itself has been a fortified iron age camp, an Acropolis for the Greeks of Marseille, a Roman fort and, during the middle ages, a citadel of the Counts of Provence and the Kings of Aragon.

At the foot of the castle the **Old Town** spreads itself out between Paillon and the Mediterranean. It is unquestionably the most picturesque part of the entire city. In each of its highly coloured alleyways can be found houses that cover the entire spectrum from white ochre to red ochre. The streets of the old town, like its many stairways, climb, twist, turn and descend through the crowded district of la *Boucherie*, *le Marché*, *la Loge* and *Les Voûtes* where the delightful, sing song accents of the local populace can be heard everywhere. Rambling through the area, the visitor will stumble upon the **Place St-François** with its 18th century Town Hall, or the flower market of the **Cours Saléya**. Here, of a morning, a profusion of colours and perfumes greets the visitor; while in the evening the terraces of cafés and restaurants provide a cheerful and spirited atmosphere in which to mingle. The nearby **Opera House** is also worth a detour.

Preparations in la Socca.

▲ *The streets of Old Nice.*

The Saint Réparate Cathedral. ▶

The 17th century **Saint-Réparate Cathedral** designed by the local architect *André Guibera* is the jewel of the Old Town. Its two-storey façade is in a neo-classical style and the church tower dates from the 18th century. The interior is built in the form of a Latin cross, with a central dome and three naves. The church houses the mitre of Saint Bassus, as well as a reliquary associated with Saint Victor. The *Rue de la Préfecture* joins the old town to the rest of the city.

Views of Old Nice. ▼

The main artery of the city is Jea Médecin Avenue, named after a forme mayor of Nice. Here can be found th imposing **Basilique de Notre Dame** in neo-gothic style reminiscent of Notre Dame de Paris. The avenue opens o into the **Place Masséna**, remarkable fe the harmony achieved by its architectu al ensemble in red ochre. Every year, a Carnival time, the square becomes a open-air theatre. The sumptuous ga dens and superb fountains bordering th square complete the perfect picture. It the true heart of the open spaces whic start at the **Promenade des Anglai** pass through the **Albert the First Ga dens** and stretch to the remarkable cu tural ensemble comprising the **Theatr** the **Musée d'Art Moderne et d'A Contemporain** and the **Acropolis**.

▲ *Water jets from the fountain in the Place Masséna.*

The Basilica of Our Lady.

▲ *The markets of Old Nice.*

▲ *Café terraces in the Cours Saleya.*

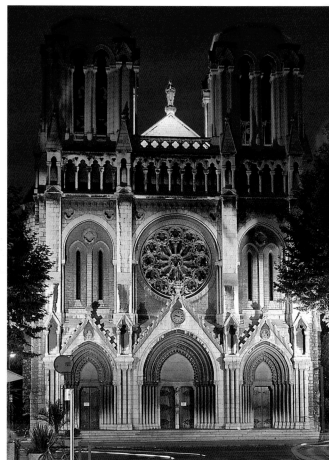

Interior of the Russian Church. ▲

The Royal Door with access to the altar. ▼

...mong the many religious buildings in Nice ... is worth mentioning the **Church of Je**
...us, which has a neo-classical façade and ... single nave, it was dedicated to Saint-
...acques at the beginning of the 18th cen
...ury. Also notable are the **Chapelle de l'An-**
...onciation, dedicated to Saint James and
...e 18th century Church of the **Virgin of**
...Mercy whose vault was painted by *Bistolfi*.
...he **Russian Church** located in the
...roximity of the Boulevard *Tzarewitch*.
...onstructed between 1903 and 1914 in
...ccordance with the plans of the archi
...ect *Preobrajenski* its external structure is
...eminiscent of the church of Saint Basil in
...Moscow. The interior is notable for its
...alls painted with frescoes by *Designori*
...rom designs by *Pianovski*. It has a single
...ave with an incredible abundance of
...onography: an image of the Virgin, a
...aint Michael, an image of the Blessed

Saviour (copied from an icon in the Cathedral of the Assumption in Moscow),
Notre Dame de Kazan, a Virgin of Vladimir in bronze and a Saint Nicholas.

THE MUSEUMS

A city of culture; Nice has many museums.

The **Musée National Message Biblique Marc Chagall** is to be found on the hill of Cimiez. It was built in 1972 by the architect *A. Hermant*. Chagall became a resident of Vence in 1950 and expressed the desire to see all his works on biblical themes collected under one roof. This museum respects that wish. The seventeen works that make up the *Biblical Message* are displayed in two salons. Another vast hall houses twelve more paintings and in an adjoining room there are five more illustrating «*The Song of Songs*». There is also a beautiful, circular chamber designed to be used for conferences and concerts,

«Noah and the Rainbow» –a painting ▶ from the Biblical Message series– by Marc Chagall.

which is decorated by three large stained glass windows representing the *Creation of the World*.

The **Masséna Museum**, which is housed in a palace on the Promenade des Anglais, contains an interesting collection of ancient pictures. In one room a series of portraits of Maréchal Masséna can be admired, along with paintings of battles in which this famous son of Nice took part. Also worthy of mention are the collections of ceramics, old weapons, jewellery, oriental clothing, some paintings showing Garibaldi, a bust of Masséna in marble –the work of *Canova*– and a statue of Napoleon.

The Masséna Museum: the outside of the museum, room dedicated to Masséna and a First Empire style bedroom.

◀ The Russian Orthodox Cathedral.

▲ *Detail of the sumptuous staircase in the Lascaris Palace.*

The **Musée Lascaris**, in Rue Droite, i housed in a Genovese style palace tha once belonged to the Lascaris-Vintimill family. The palace was the seat of th Revolutionary Tribunal from 1792 t 1794. Pride of place here is «L'Etag Noble» (the majestic staircase) and o the ground floor can be found a phar macy from 1738 which has preserve its collection of tripods and jars.

The **Musée Matisse**, housed in a small C miez palace, was founded in 1963. In it ar preserved a variety of objects that onc belonged to the painter, along with hi paintings: *Odalisque*, *A Portrait of Laurett* and *Still Life with Reader at a Yellow Table*

▲ *The Old Pharmacy in the Lascaris Palace.*

▼ *A room in the Matisse Museum.*

Exhibition rooms at
the Naval Museum.

▲ *The Chéret Museum: «She», a painting by G.A. Mossa.*

The **Musée des Beaux Arts Jules Chéret** on the Avenue des Beaumettes, houses paintings from European schools from the 17th to 19th century. Among the works on display are pictures by *Van Loo*, *Natoire*, *Fragonard* and a large selection of French Masters from the 19th century: *Besnard*, *Blanche*, *Cabanel*, *Couture*, *Flameng*, etc. There are also sculptures by *Carpeaux* and *Rodin*, ceramics by *Picasso* and an important collection of impressionists including works by: *Monet*, *Sisley*, *Renoir*, *Degas*, *Guiaumin*, *Dufy*, *Van Dongen* and *Survage*. Numerous paintings by local Nice artist *G.A. Mossa* are also on display.

The other museums in Nice are the **Archaeological Museum**, within the grounds of the Roman City, the **Prehistory Museum** and the **Maritime Museum**.

In the upper town can be found Roman ruins and the **Monastery of Cimiez** whose church contains some beautiful masterpieces. Both sites are well worth a visit.

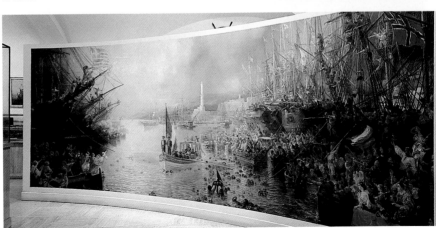

▲ *The Monastery at Chiviez: the façade and the altar.*

◄ *The arenas at Cimiez.*

The **Nice Carnival** is famous throughout the world. Its origins go back at least as far as the 13th century; though its current form follows a tradition established in 1873.

Throughout the festivities, parades by the King of Carnival alternate with battles of flowers rich in colour and scents.

The participants spend the entire year building floats, costumes and Big Head masks, all to create the enchanted world that is Carnival.

The spectacle of the Place Masséna sumptuously decorated and magnificiently lit for the festivities is a sight not to be missed.

▲ *The marine complex at Baie des Anges.*

VILLENEUVE-LOUBET

Villeneuve-Loubet is situated on the River Loup, at the foot of a medieval castle, which is itself dominated by a 33 metre high pentagonal tower. It was here that the peace treaty of Nice was signed in 1538.

The town was the hometown of *August Escoffier* (1846-1935) «Chef to King and King of Chefs». A **Museum of th Culinary Arts** has been created in th house where he was born. There can b found works written by the master che himself, along with an interesting collec tion of kitchen utensils and recip books. The wine cellar, in a natural cave plays host to some of the great Pro vence wines.

The **Musée Militaire**, dedicated princ pally to the conflicts of the 20th centur gives civilians a chance to learn abou diverse uniforms and weapons.

Along the sea front, the **Marina Bai des Anges** extends its strangely con toured buildings throughout the yach ing harbour. The architect *Andr Minagoy* designed them during th 1970s.

◀ *Aerial view of Port-St-Laurent.*

CAGNES-SUR-MER

There are, in fact, three towns which go to make up Cagnes-sur-Mer: the **Cros-de-Cagnes** on the seafront, **Le Logis**, the modern commercial town and boosting in the upper reaches, the **Haut-de-Cagnes**.

This latter mentioned area is a medieval village that occupies a privileged position offering a remarkable panorama. Its characteristic houses, dotted all round the Castle, line the narrow twisting streets and are decorated with flowers. The whole area being ringed by 13th century ramparts. A Visit to the Castle is interesting, as much for the richness of its internal decoration, as for the diversity of museum material it houses. The Castle also plays its part in the culture of the area, since it is here that an annual International Festival of Painting, created by *Jean-Clergue*, is held.

It is impossible to speak of Cagnes, without mentioning *Auguste Renoir* who lived here from 1907 until his death in 1919. The house he had built, in the Collettes district of the town, is today a museum dedicated to his life and art.

The town also has a famous racecourse, to be found near the sea.

The beaches of Cagnes-sur-Mer.

Haut-de-Cagnes. ▲

The Castle Museum. ▼   *The ascent to Bourgade.* ▼

▲ *A medieval street in Haut-de-Cagnes.*

General view of Biot.

A picturesque passageway. ▲

BIOT

A picturesque village sat atop a hill overlooking the Brague valley. Biot is considerably rich in sites of interest to the tourist. In the first instance there is the 12th century **Place des Arcades** whose beautiful arches span the square at the heart of the village.

The portal of the nearby **Romanesque Church** dates from 1506 and was created by *Tadeus Nigerus*. In the interior of the building are two altarpieces of the *Brea* school (1500). One, having eight sections, represents the Virgin of the Rosary surrounded by saints. The other, whose central figure is an «*Ecce Homo*», has four sections.

Biot is rich in deposits of sand, clay and manganese, which from time immemorial have been shaped by local potters and baked into jars. The Phoenicians once exported their products from the nearby port of Antibes.

For years now, the reputation of Biot has been growing, thanks to its artisans working in glass. These craftsmen, using time-honoured techniques, make carafes, glasses, bottles, jugs and all kinds of decorative objects. Biot is also an important production centre for roses and carnations.

A mere six kilometres from the village, in Saint Pierre, can be found **The Fernand Léger Museum**. *Léger* was a great French painter and a friend of *Picasso* and *Braque*. The American art critic *Sweeney* called him «The Modern Primitive». The façade of the building is decorated with a brightly coloured mosaic. In the interior there is a collection of drawings, paintings, tapestries and ceramics by the artist, illustrating his personal evolution from 1904 to 1955, including his passage through cubism. As any visitor will no doubt testify, he really was an extraordinarily expressive painter.

Glass Craftsmanship. ▶

The Place des Arcades. ▶

From Nice to Antibes

▲ *An alleyway behind the ramparts.*

▼ *Aerial view of the port and the old town.*

ANTIBES

At the opposite end of the Baie de Anges from Nice is the ancient port of Antibes. Founded by the Phoenicians in the 4th century BC, its name derived from its geographical position opposit –«*Antipolis*»– Nice. From the 5th century, the Greeks of Massalia established chain of merchants who traded with the Ligurian tribes. Although well protected within its ramparts, which run from the cove of Salis to that of Saint Roch Antibes was a port of call that was always at the mercy of Ligurian raids Two centuries later, it had become Roman municipal borough with a barracks and an arsenal. Later, barbarian invasions destroyed the town. From the 14th century onwards the French king were only too aware of the strategic importance of Antibes, especially when it formed part of the frontier between France and Savoy.

The Square Fort.

ach reign was to improve the fortifications, raised by *Vauban*. Though little remains of them today except for the **Fort Carré** (square fort) and the sea front ramparts. In 1794, Bonaparte took charge of the defence of the coast and installed his family in the fort. Robespierre was imprisoned here for quite some time, after his fall from grace. General *Championnet*, who had played such an illustrious role in the Italian and German campaigns died in Antibes in 1800. His last wish was to be buried in the grave pits of Fort Carré. A bust of the general erected in the **Cours Masséna** preserves his memory for posterity. Antibes was the birthplace of Maréchal Reille (1775-1860) who distinguished himself in the Napoleonic campaigns before coming over to the side of the monarchy and being named Maréchal by Louis-Phillipe.

The streets of old Antibes. ▶

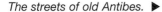

The Grimaldi Castle and some pieces from the Picasso Museum.

The narrow streets, decked with flower of the old town, lead the visitor to th **Château Grimaldi**, originally built, as Roman Fort, on a terrace overlooking th sea. Rebuilt in the 16th century, it st preserves its Roman Square and Roma Tower. The château currently houses th **Musée Picasso,** which has an ine timable collection of paintings, drawing engravings, lithographs and ceramic created by the celebrated artist. The are also some interesting archaeologic finds on display, while out on the terrac overlooking the sea, four statues k *Germaine Richier* can be admired.

◀ *The ramparts from the route to Cap.*

The ramparts of Antibes. ▲

A passageway in the old town. ▶

From Nice to Antibes

▲ *Islet Point at Cap d'Antibes.*

Among other important sites worthy of mention are the 17th century **Cathedral**, with its Romanesque apse and transept and a magnificent altarpiece from the *Louis Bréa* School, which dates from 1515.

Located in the Bastion of Saint Andrew, part of the Vauban fortifications, the **Musée Archéologique** has an important collection of coins and antique ceramics evoking the long history of Antibes. The **Musée Naval et Napoléonien** is housed in a fortified round tower known as the Batterie de Grillon, which is located at the South-easternmost point of the Cap d'Antibes. Behind the church and the castle can be found the sea front boulevard which is, in fact, a well preserved section of the 12th century ramparts and from which a fine view can be had of Nice and the Alpine chain. At the harbour can be found the **Porte Marine**, close to which is a fountain erected by Louis 16th in honour of *General d'Aguillon* who had repaired the Roman aqueducts supplying the town with water.

The Napoleonic and Naval Museum.

The Vauban port. ▲

odern Antibes is a major production
entre for cut flowers (roses, carnations,
nd anemones). Nearly 800 horticultural
ompanies take up a surface area of
ome three million square metres.
ntibes has the distinction of being the
lace where the Eucalyptus was grown
nd acclimatised for the first time in
urope.

he creation of the renowned **Port de
laisance** (the Yachting Harbour) and a
xury golf course (near Biot) are recent
ajor tourist developments. Also of
ote, four kilometres away from An-
bes, is **Marineland**, reputedly the best
arine park in Europe. In its many pools
wim dolphins, killer whales, seals and
tters, etc.

Marineland aquatic park. ▶

▲ *Juan-les-Pins.*

JUAN-LES-PINS

Beyond the Cap d'Antibes, this Spa Resort elegantly extends the modern town of Antibes. Juan-les-Pins was created on the sole initiative of American millionaire F.J. Goul and has been developing ever since 1925. Its beach of fine sand, surrounded by a floral embankment, is one of its main tourist attractions. The terraces of the **Casino** dominate the beach, offering magnificent views out over the Golfe-Juan, the Île Sainte-Marguerite and L'Esterel. A well-known *Jazz Festival* is held here every year, in the pinewood at the edge of the sea.

▲ *Re-enactment of Napoleon's embarkation at Golfe-Juan.*

GOLFE-JUAN

Golfe-Juan stretches across a vast ba between Juan-les-Pins and Canne Lush green hills carpeted in flower orange groves, pines and eucalyptu dominate the town. It was here th Napoleon landed, on the 1st of Marc 1815, after his escape from Elba. plaque in the *Avenue De la Gare* and column topped by a bust in *Nabonnar Square* commemorate the event.

The eastern part of the town contai the old fishing port and the mode yachting harbour, ringed by an attrac tive promenade which also passes the installations of the *Camillon Rayo Port*; the quays and wharves of whic can provide berths for 800 boats. Th Port is also home to lively shops, re taurants and beaches and the *Théât de la Mer*, all of which adds to th dynamism of what the town can off tourists. A well-protected natural ha bour, with long beaches covered in fi sand, invites the visitor to experienc the joys of sailing, to take a swim, or try underwater diving. (There is a underwater cavern of some 27 metre at *Huet*).

◄ *The port at Golfe-Juan.*

VALLAURIS

An important pottery centre, Vallauris had its name intrinsically linked in the 20th century to **Picasso**. The great artist came here to live after the Second World War and gave new fame to the already celebrated local ceramics industry. Picasso painted a monumental mural in the marvellous **Chapelle Romane**. He also gave the town a group of sculptures entitled *L'Homme au Mouton*, (sheep man) which is to be found in the Place Paul Isnard.

The Gallo-Romans had made use of the clay deposits of the region, but the true tradition of pottery and ceramics in the area did not really begin until the 16th century. After the village had been devastated by the plague it was repopulated by 70 families from the Genovese Riviera, among whom were potters who began to make objects for domestic use. The crafting of ceramics for artistic purposes began in the middle of the 19th century. *Jacques Messier* was one of the grand masters of the art. Production intensified and other great potters emerged such as *Louis Pezzetto*, *Lévy Dhumes*, *Charles Lévêque*, and *Père Sauvan*. The industry went through a period of great development at the end of the 19th century and then into something of a decline. However, it was given a boost by the presence of Picasso, who also fostered the rediscovery and general reassessment of ceramics. Today there are some 200 workshops producing a vast quantity of useful and decorative objects.

Some potteries at Vallauris.

«Sheep Man» by Picasso. ▲

The town centre. ▼

▲ *The waterfall at Courmes.*

▲ *The Pont-du-Loup (Wolf's Bridge).*

GORGES DE LOUP

The source of the River Loup is in the alpine foothills, 1,300 metres up at Grasse and along its journey to the sea it passes through numerous pictu-resque villages. However, it is difficult to believe when contemplating the Loup

▼ *The road following the Loup.*

◄ *The bottom of the Gorges.*

languorously disgorging into the blu Mediterranean that on its way there had carved huge gorges out of the livin rock, producing, as it did so, one of th most beautiful natural curiosities in th whole Provence region.

Pont de Loup, a small town, famous fc its fruit jams, marks the entrance into th Gorges. These incredible ravines wer gouged by tumultuous torrents thrustin through the limestone rocks. To acces the chasms, the visitor has to pass th pillars and vaults of a superb viaduc –lamentably destroyed in 1944– whic used to carry the train from Provenc The Gorges are carved vertically an crossed by enormous bowls forming superb composite. In a semicircular ho low, the **Cascade de Courmes**, the rive leaps vertically up as it plunges down th limestone rock face. A few hundred me tres higher, at the outlet of a tunnel, is th waterfall known as the **Saut de Lou** (wolf's leap) where the river cascade joyfully among an abundant vegetation.

Gourdon, perched on the rock. ▲

GOURDON

Built on top of a rocky spur some 800 metres high, this veritable eagle's nest of a feudal village occupies a remarkable site overlooking the Gorges de Loup. An ancient Saracen fort, Gourdon has preserved the charm of its past through its antiquated houses looking onto ancient streets and through its 14th century castle.

The main street of the village leads to a tiny square that is a veritable viewing platform for the Riviera, offering an exceptional panorama looking out towards Nice and beyond to the Mont de l'Estérel. Around these lofty heights often circle Hang-gliders and Para-gliders like huge coloured birds outlined against the azure sky.

The main street. ▲
The entrance to the village. ▼

The Eagle's Nest. ▶

The Loup Region

▲ Bar-sur-Loup.

▲ Statue of the Admiral of Grasse in front of the Church at Bar-sur-Loup.

▲ The Church of La Colle.

◄ La Colle-sur-Loup.

A street in Tourettes. ▶

OURETTES-SUR-LOUP

spended on the flanks of the moun-
in, the outer houses of Tourettes
pear to form a rampart. Remarkably
ell preserved, the village has a 15th
ntury church with works from the
onardo da Vinci School and a triptych
Bréa. It also has a number of carved
ures of Saints in polychrome wood
d sculpted wooden panelling from the
th century. The majestic **Châteu
arré** is adorned with magnificent Louis
lth balustrades. There is also a fine
ew from here looking out towards
nce and Grasse.
merous artisans have set up shop in
e town, seduced by the charm of its
cient stones, adding their production
the local harvest of olives, carnations,
ses, anemones and, above all, violets,
ich furnish the town's annual fete
th one of the most prized floral dis-
ays on the Riviera.

The Violet Festival. ▶

General view of Tourettes-sur-Loup. ▼   *A vaulted passageway in the old village.* ▶

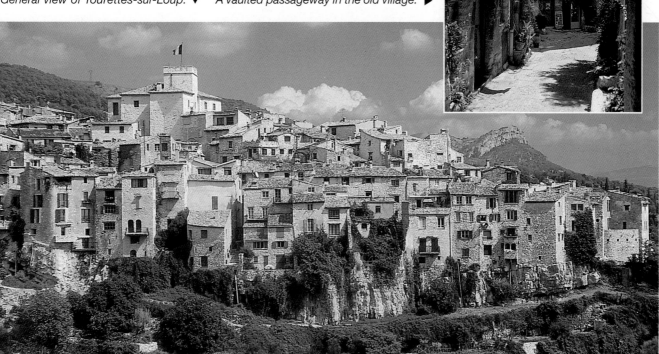

▲ *A florid street in old Vence.*

▼ *General view.*

VENCE

This quintessential tourist city encom passes a medieval centre in which glimpses of its rich history can still b seen. Founded by the Ligurians, it wa subservient to the Romans from the 2n century BC on, but developed on i own with the coming of Christianity. steadily grew in power and became a Episcopal town in the 4th century, whic it remained until 1789. It is astonishin the number of leading Bishops wh once commanded this tiny bishopri the smallest in France. They includ *Saint-Véran* in the 5th century; *Sair Lambert* in the 12th century; the Italia prince *Alexandre Farnese*, who becam Pope under the name Paul III; the writ *Antoine Godeau* –the first to be appoir ed to the *Académie Française* t Richlieu– who took his assignment se ously and did much to develop th activities of Vence «perfume makir tanning and pottery» and finally *Jea. Baptiste Surian* in the 18th century. T bishops of Vence were almost constar ly at loggerheads with the feudal lorc of the city, the Barons of Villeneuve.

The Chapel of the Rosary. ▲

The fountain at Peyra.

The Chapel of the Penitents. ▲

nce, a city of the arts, has a **thedral** with a tumultuous past. Built a rise on which a pagan temple, a erovingian sanctuary, and a Carolin- an church had been previously sited, e Cathedral underwent many modifi- tions from the 15th to the 17th centu- . Today it houses numerous re- arkable works of art.

visit to the **Chapel of the Rosary** corated by Henri Matisse in appreci- ion of the medical treatment the ominican sisters had given him, is a erequisite. The artist designed all of e decoration (paintings, furniture, litur- cal objects, stained glass, etc).

The old town, with its «*à pontis*» streets (arched passageways), its ancient gates, its fountains, its little squares –like the *Place de Frêne* with its ma- jestic tree– has preserved all of its authenticity. There is also a wonderful view available from the *Place Thiers* over the valley of *Lubiane* and out towards the Alps.

A picturesque street. ▲

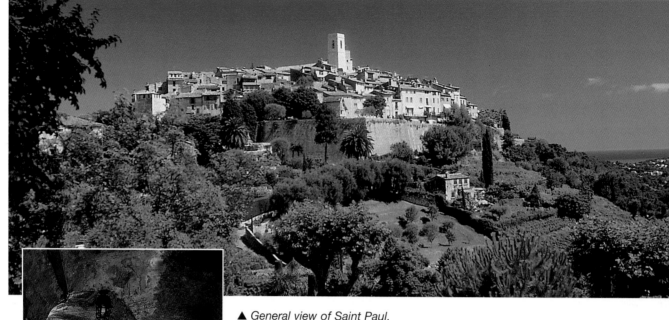

▲ *General view of Saint Paul.*

◀ *A vaulted passageway.*

SAINT-PAUL DE VENCE

Once an ancient fortress that defended the frontier of Var, Saint-Paul de Vence towers over a magnificent landscape that extends all the way to the sea. From the height of its walls the views are superb. The light has a particular quality here and distinctly illuminates the surrounding cypresses, citrus trees, vines, mimosas and bougainvillae The feudal structure of the town has pr served all of its authenticity. The encl sure is entered by passing under the ar of the massive 16th century tower, guar ed by cannon. This tower was built on t orders of François the First to defend t village against the Dukes of Savoy.

Saint-Paul was even, at one time, a roy borough, which depended directly the kings of France. The town enter on the historical stage in the 10th cent ry when *Roméo de Villeneuve* annexe Saint-Paul to the territory of Roquefo Queen Jeanne, the daughter of Robe de Provence, the king of Naples, alli with Pope Clement VI at the time of conflict with Louis of Hungary. S granted him the castle of Avignon. the death of Queen Jeanne, Saint-Pa passed into the hands of the Duke Anjou who confirmed the privileges the town and also conferred lord jurisprudence on Roquefort ar Tourettes. The village, became a fortifi town under François the First, wh destroyed the earlier, ancient fortific tions and rebuilt them anew in 1537.

◀ *View over the western ramparts.*

int-Paul has an extraordinary rich-
ss of sights, in which pride of place
ust go to the **Collégiale de la
nversion de Saint Paul** flanked by
square steeple. The church, con-
ucted between the 12th and 13th
ntury, was rebuilt in the 18th century.
did not become a Collégiale (learning
ntre) until 1666. It is basically Gothic
style, with some later additions. In the
erior the visitor can admire three
autiful masterpieces: the splendid
th century image of the Virgin in sil-
r; a 14th century cross used in pro-
ssions and a Saint Catherine by
ntoretto, as well as a 15th century reli-
ary of Saint Anthony.

St Claire's Chapel. ▶

The Collegiate School.

Some picturesque views of the village. ▲

The Loup Region

In the main square there is the urn shaped **Grand Fountain** dating from 1850 and a vaulted arched washhouse. Rambling down the **Main Street**, which links the two gates of the city, or through the neighbouring streets, is a constantly changing pleasure. It is at once a voyage of architectural discovery into the town's past through the contemplation of its well preserved façades, as well as an immersion into the cultural world of the abundant art galleries, which are there to explore. Crafts shops, and shops selling local produce, complete the décor and contribute to the undeniable charm of Saint-Pau which houses –as might be expected– the **Musée Provenç** A permanent theatrical even can be w nessed outside its ramparts in t **Place Charles De Gaull**e as young a old compete in the ancient game *pétanque* or boules; it is a local insti tion whose origins go back to ti immemorial. Also of interest is the ce brated hostel the «**Colombe d'**((golden dove) where so many celebrit have spent the night. It may be cons ered an art gallery in its own rig thanks to the magnificent private coll tion of 20th century paintings it p ssesses. On its walls can be found wo by *Picasso*, *Matisse*, *Dufy*, *Derain*, *Utr* and many other well-known artists.

◀ *The Main Street.*
▼ *The Grand Fountain.*

A street in the village. ▲

he MAEGHT Foundation

'ithin Saint-Paul de Vence, on the summit of a hill, the
aeght Foundation is one of the most interesting modern art
useums in the world. Constructed in brick, steel and glass,
was designed by the Catalan architect Josep Lluis Sert. The
useum, which owes its name to its celebrated founders
'mé and Marguerite Maeght, was inaugurated in 1964 by
ndré Malraux. At the entrance, the visitor is greeted by a
obile-immobile piece by Calder. The Foundation houses a
rodigious collection of contemporary works. The structure,
d the internal and external lay out of the building, confer on
a feeling that it is a living space, a hub of art and culture.
mong the numerous artists with work on display are
andinsky, Braque, Marc Chagall, Miró, Matisse, Léger,
onnard and Giacometti.

Giacometti sculptures in the Maeght Foundation. ▶

▲ *General view.*

GRASSE

Grasse is a welcoming, picturesque resort town on an outstanding site. It began to attract to tourists as early as the 19th century, who came here to enjoy its climate.

The main industry of the town today, as it has been for centuries, is perfume making of which it is the World Capital. Although the distillation of aromatic essences began in the 13th century, it became more industrialised in the 16th century when the Medici made perfumed gloves fashionable. Ten thousand tons of flowers are currently processed annually in Grasse. The essential oils allow for the manufacture of aromas used in the perfume industry. In honour of this industry, which has given the city its riches and renown, there is a **Musée International de la Parfumerie** in which our passion for perfumes over the last four hundred years is superbly presented.

andering around the **Old Town**, rough its serpentine streets and up d down its carved steps, the visitor is und to find the **Place aux Aires** with arcades, its buildings with 18th cenry façades and its magnificent founns. Along with the market, it is the eliest part of the city.

e most important architectural feare in the city is the **Cathedral de tre Dame du Puy**, built in the 12th ntury and restored in the 17th centu-. The restoration added the double t of steps leading up to the entrance, th its long stone ramp, and the crypt. side the church there are three intings by *Rubens* as well as «The ashing of the feet» by *Fragonard*, he mystical marriage of Saint Caerine» by *Sébastien Bourdon* and the traordinary altarpiece attributed to uis Bréa.

ose by, there is the **Jardin de la incess Pauline**, the **Petit Paris ospital** –whose chapel contains three intings by *Natoire*– and the **Corniche blic Park**.

The fountain in the Place aux Aires. ▶

The Cathedral of Our Lady. ▲

The Grasse Region

▲ A street in the old town.

◀ The distillery and laboratory of the perfume makers Molinar

▼ The market in the Place aux Aires.

he painter **Fragonard** was born in
rasse in 1732. A museum bearing his
ame is housed in a magnificent 18th
entury residence, which once belong-
d to the *Marquise de Cabris*. Within its
arvellous rooms can be seen canvas-
s with erotic motifs that were thrown
ut by *Madame du Barry* and hidden in
rasse by Fragonard during the period
f the Revolution.

Vertiginous view of the Cathedral. ▲
The Fragonard Museum: a portrait of the painter and 18th and 19th century salons. ▼

The Grasse Region

CABRIS

350 metres high and 30 kilometres from the sea, the ancient village of Cabris offers the visitor one of the best panoramas of the Riviera. The vista sweeps from Cap Ferrat to the foothills near Toulon; while looking out toward the Îles de Lérins, the view recedes into infinity. Dominated by its 10th century castle, the origins of the town go way back to the year 400 AD. These days, thanks to a craft revival, the town has rediscovered its ancient industry: pottery. Cabris enjoys a mild climate and is a very pleasant tourist resort.

A few kilometres from the town, at the St-Cassien Lake, all manner of aquatic sports may be practised.

◀ *Lake St-Cassien.*

General view of Cabris.

▲ *Saint-Cézaire.*

PEYMEINADE

Located some 20 kilometres from the sea amidst olive groves and fields of cultivated flowers, this charming Provençal town clings to the foot of the Cabris Mountain. Surrounded by numerous picturesque hamlets the houses of the old village are grouped around the 17th century church. Peymeinade has been experiencing rapid development recently as it offers a wide range of possibilities for doing sport or just relaxing and is an exclusive holiday centre.

SAINT-CEZAIRE SUR SIAGNE

Fifteen kilometres to the west of Grasse is Saint-Cezaire, a small village 500 metres high on the edge of a plateau dominating the **Siagne**. The village has preserved its feudal lay out, centred on its Castle and a 12th century Romanesque Chapel. A splendid view is available from the town, which takes in the Monts de Tanneron, L'Estérel, the Îles de Lérins, Cannes and Mougins.

The principal tourist attraction in the area is the **caves** carved out of the limestone over millennia and discovered in the 19th century. The caves descend some 50 metres and extend some 20 metres into the interior of the rock and enjoy a constant temperature, all year round, of 14° C. They are remarkable for the variety and abundance of their limestone forms, sculpted by the unimaginable fantasy of nature over the centuries. The stalagmites and stalactites are red in colour, due to the presence of iron oxides and abundant with simulacra in the shape of coral, flowers, stars and animals. They are also surprisingly musical.

▼ *A street in old Peymeinade.*

La Place des Arcades at Valbonne.

ALBONNE

...king full advantage of the arrival in the ...ea of leading businesses of Sophia-An-...olis, Valbonne has been going through ... extraordinary development phase. ...ew housing, a new town hall, a new ...blic auditorium, new schools and new ...ops have rapidly overwhelmed this ...aint old village on the edge of a forest ...hich had only just left behind its tradi-...nal agrarian economy, thrusting it firmly ...to the milieu of the twenty-first century. ...albonne has monastic foundations. ...ollowing on from the work of the Monks ... the Lérins, the Chalasien monks of the

Abbey of Prads, founded an abbey here in 1189 and named the place «**Vallis Bonna**». The very beautiful church, situated at the south of the village, where the River Brague flows, was the chapel of the ancient monastery. In 1519, *Augustin de Grimaldi* decided to rebuild the village along strictly symmetrical lines. The streets are all at right angles, forming a kind of checker board around the lovely central square ringed with tall 17th century houses atop arcades. Not too far from here, water seems to have flowed forever in the ancient bathtub shaped drinking fountain in front of the ancient town hall.

A street in Châteauneuf-de-Grasse. ▼

HATEAUNEUF-DE-GRASSE

...tuated on top of a mound, this superb, ...eaceful Provençal village appears to ...ve chosen to turn its back on the ...usy Cagnes to Grasse main road that ...ns nearby, so as to be better able to ...en its heart as a true balcony over-...oking the Gulf of Napoule. Here, high ...d buildings, narrow streets and tran-...il little squares give the village its ...arm and its particular character.

The village of Opio. ▲

OPIO

The «*oppidum*» (raised field), which gave its name to the town, along with the plain below it, have existed for aeons atop a promontory between Chatêauneuf and Grasse. For many of those centuries, the principal resources of Opio have been olives, table grapes and plants destined for use in making perfumes. The village's olive oil mill is still operating, as it has done now for five hundred years. The majority of the village's inhabitants today live on the plain, which has gone through a spectacular development of late offering a multitude of leisure activities to holiday makers from all points of the compass. The Club Méditérranée and the local Golf Course have added to Opio's fame as a resort.

MOUANS-SARTOUX

Nowadays, Mouans-Sartoux is a expanding, busy, commercial villag mid-way between Cannes and Gras: on the Route Napoleon. However, the: two ancient feudal hamlets were d serted at the end of the Middle Age then repopulated in 1496. They ke their separate identities, until they we fused together into a village, under o double-barrelled name, by imper decree in 1818. The narrow streets co form to a rectilinear plan, always cros ing at right angles. The 17th, 18th ar 19th century houses have porches ar are remarkably well preserved. Trimme with an attractive shady park ar flanked by three towers, the **Castle** Mouans is an exquisite 16th centu building that has been very w restored.

▲ *The Castle at Mouans-Sartoux.*
▼ *An old fountain in Mougins.*

The Automobile Museum of Mougins is just off the A8 Motorway, between Antibes and Cannes (Bréguières services).
It has a collection of antique, luxury and racing vehicles on show which is one of the most complete and attractive in Europe. The permanent exhibition has more than a hundred, famous make, vehicles dating from 1894 to the present.

General view of the old village.

A picturesque street. ▼

The Chapel of Our Lady of Life. ▲

¹OUGINS

ⁱerched at 250 metres between Cannes ᵗd Grasse, this ancient fortified bor-ᵘgh has a very picturesque outline. ʳst occupied by the Ligurians, it was ᵗer conquered by the Romans. The ori-ⁿ of the name of the town is polemical ᵐong historians; some believe it comes ᵒm *Mons Aighitnae*, while others claim ᵈerives from *Mons Germinus*.

ᵒugins once belonged to the Abbey of ᵉrins and played an important role in ᵉ history of the area during the Middle ᵍes. As witnesses of its former glory it ᵃs preserved some ramparts and a ⁵th century fortified gate. The main ʳchitectural monument, however, is the ᵃrish Church, began in the 11th centu-ᵗ. The steeple dominates a splendid ᵃnoramic view from l'Estérel to the Îles ᵉ Lérins and the foothills of the Alps. In ᵉ Place Sainte-Anne there is a com-ᵉmorative bust of Commander Lamy, ᵗe of the town's most illustrious sons, ᵗo fell gloriously, in 1900, on the ᵃnks of the Shari in Africa.

The **Chapel of Our Lady of Life** can be found some ten minutes from the town centre. This ancient sanctuary was founded in the 12th century. It is sur-rounded by cypresses and was chosen as their final resting-place by the monks of Saint-Honorat. During the Middle Ages, Notre-Dame-de-Vie was a major site for pilgrimages in the Provence area. It is now an important tourist centre, having successfully preserved its quiet atmosphere, its particular character, its magnificent Provence style houses and its sumptuous parks, unwinding around its stepped terraces. A number of establishments with great gastronomic reputations add to the attraction of the town for visitors.

Cannet Town Hall.

▲
▼ *Some views of old Cannet.*

LE CANET-ROCHEVILLE

Surrounded by hills, this important tow
is located in a privileged position ar
benefits from very pleasant, mild se
breezes. Founded by the monks
Lérens, Le Cannet is an ideal locatic
for those who adore tranquillity. She
tered by the *Pézou* and the *Tete c
Guillet*, the residential area is some 25
metres above sea level. It is a town tha
has conserved many monuments to i
illustrious past. These include th
Eglise de Sainte-Catherine, the **O
Lady of the Angels** and the **Penitent
chapels, the 15th century **Brigand
Tower** and the **Calvis Tower**.

Among the famous people who were born, in Cannet we can mention *Curé Arsson* (1660-1731) –who reorganised the defence of the town against the troops of Eugène de Savoy– and *A.L. Sardou*, the historian and father of the great writer Victorien Sardou. It was in Cannet that the great tragedian Rachel died in 1858. The painters Pierre Bonnard and Henri Labasque once lived here and the Agha Khan had a villa built here which dominates the town. Moreover, Le Cannet is a cultural town where various events, such as the Grand Prix de Poésie (a poetry competition), the Orange Tree Fair and numerous exhibitions of paintings take place.

Cannet: from little streets to modern avenues.

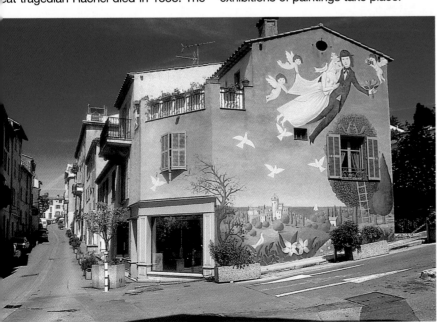

Cannes and the surrounding area

▲ Palms on La Croisette.
▼ The Casino.

CANNES

Built on the site of an ancient Liguri
city, on an elevation that slopes down
the edge of the Gulf of Napoule a
with a backdrop of the Massif of L'E
térel, it is difficult to imagine a mc
splendid location than that of Canne
Sheltered by its surrounding hills, th
privileged area enjoys a mild and ter
perate climate.

Among the famous festivals held he
probably the most celebrated is t
International Festival of Cinema whi
helps make Cannes one of the mc
often visited cities in the world. The o
gins of the city are little known, since
languished in obscurity for centuri
until 1834. That was the year that *Lo
Brougham*, who was the British Lc
Chancellor at the time, was en route
Italy when a cholera outbreak the
forced him to make an unschedul
stop over in Cannes. Impressed by t
mild climate, the blue of the sky and t
beauty of the site he decided to build
winter residence there and numero
British aristocrats followed his examp
Lord Brougham obtained the fun
needed to build a dike besides the c
town from King Louis Phillipe. The tov
continued to grow from then on until
became the world famous resort it
today.

Sandy Beaches.

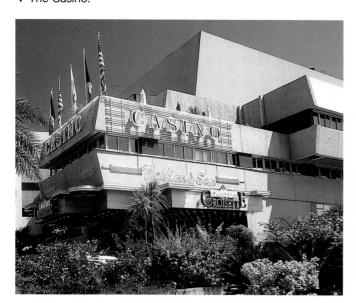

Aerial View. ▲
The beach at Gray d'Albion. ▼

hile Cannes was no more than a peaceful little fishing village for centuries, the **Iles de Lérins**, Saint-Marguerite and Saint-Honorat, which face out in the bay, were of major historical importance. One of these islands appears to have once been an important commercial port and also the seat of a pagan cult. According to the historian Polybe (2nd century BC), the region, whose capital Egitna was situated where Cannes is today, was occupied by the Oxibiens, a tough, hard-working, farming people who were also fond of fishing and piracy. It was their raids on Antipoles (modern Antibes) and Nice, then Greek colonies of Marseilles, which caused the inhabitants to call on the aid of the Romans to re-conquer and destroy Egitna.

In 155 BC, Marseille built the *Castrum Marcellinuium* around the elevation. Some centuries later, when the region was already colonised, two Anchorite Monks Honorat and Capraïs took refuge in L'Estérel and later on the islands of Lero and Lérina, known today as Sainte-Marguerite and Saint-Honorat. According to popular legend the second of these islands was invaded by snakes, which were actually demonic incarnations. Thanks to divine intervention, Honorat arranged for an immense tidal wave to sweep over the island and wash them all to the bottom of the sea. He himself escaped the deluge by cling-

▲ *Sunset over La Croisette.*

▲ *View over La Croisette Point.*

▼ *A fountain near the Allées de la Liberté.*

ing to a palm tree, which is why two
them appear on the abbey's standa
surrounding a golden cross.

During the first half of the 8th centu
the Saracens invaded the Cann
region and held it for many years. In 9
Guillaume Gruetta, the second son
the Count of Antibes seized the Îles
Lérins and gave to the Abbey the te
tories of Mandalieu, Arluc, Loubet a
Cannes. The possessions of the abbo
continued to grow and eventually, w
the blessing of the Pope, became
extensive autonomous fiefdom.

However, when the Saracens occupi
the citadel once again, the Abb
Adalbert II transformed his monaste
into a fortress and consolidated t
defences of Cannes by building,
Mount Chevalier the **Suquet Tow**
which still stands today. *Raymo*
Bérenger, the Count of Provence, th
agreed to certain franchises for Cann
and in 1131 an act confirmed the don
tion he had made to the Abbot of Léri
of the ancient Castrum Marceliniu
which from 1200 on became known
the *Castrum de Canoïs*. Despite vario
attempts at freeing it, Cannes remain
a dependency of the Abbot of Lérir
who controlled the coastline from
Napoule to Vallauris. The decline of t
Abbey of Lérins came in the 15th cent
ry when the ancient ecclesiastical fie
dom, which included the isles, w
handed over, by royal decree, to Prin
Joinville, the Duke of Vendôme and

her great lords. Since Province had t its independence towards the end the 15th century, the Castle of nnes was occupied by troops of uis XI. In 1580 an epidemic caused e death of two thirds of the population d in 1635 the area was the scene of ttles between the French and the anish. The latter managed to capture e islands, but were repulsed when ey tried to invade the mainland. **Fort yal**, built on Sainte-Marguerite at the e of Cardinal Richlieu, has a marvel-s view of Cannes, Antibes and the ighbouring hills. In the 18th century, nnes was completely destroyed after ving suffered several raids by Arab ates, an invasion by the troops of the ke of Savoy and finally that of the strian army.

1815 Napoleon escaped from the Isle Elbe and landed at Golfe-Juan. A all troop of forty grenadiers, under e command of *Cambronne*, then cupied Cannes and Napoleon, hid-n among the dunes, was obliged to ouac near the **Chapelle de Notre**

The market at Forville. ▲

A view over Port Canto. ▼

Cannes and the surrounding area

▲ *Aerial view of la Croisette.*

▼ *The beach of the Carlton Hotel.*

▼ *The old port and the Town Hall.*

Dame de Bon Voyage before contining on his route to Paris.

In 1858 *Prosper Mérimée*, then inspector of historic monuments, tou the Lérin Isles and noted the importar of Cannes and its surroundings. A Mérimée, who is considered the seco pioneer to discover the charms Cannes, there appeared *Guy Maupassant*, *Toqueville*, *Thiers*, *Vic Cousin* and *Stephen Liégard*, as well many other personalities from the wo of arts and letters. From this period Cannes became one of the favou haunts of artists, rich bankers, aris crats and high-class tourists. The m ern image of Cannes is well kno throughout the world. Its famous fe vals –of recorded music in January a of cinema in May– concentrate attention of music and cinema lov worldwide on the city. Numerous c gresses are held here and tourism intense throughout the year, mak Cannes a fashionable resort of tr international proportions. The city a offers extensive leisure and spo opportunities allowing the visitor to p hard too, something that is becom more fashionable than ever.

Without abandoning its traditional fet Cannes has gone out of its way to o new facilities and activities to its mu tude of visitors: a yachting harbour, g courses, polo, aquatic sports, an ae club, regattas, etc.

The flower most associated w Cannes is the mimosa, which is p

The Martinez Hotel.

The Promenade of La Croisette from Le Suquet. ▲

...ced here and exported around the ...obe. It flowers in February, giving birth ...o a festival that bears its name.

...annes stretches some nine kilometres ...m the **La Bocca** district to the rocks ...f the **Fourcade**. From the harbour the ...wn presents a wonderful panorama. ...e city is centred on the **Rue** **Antibes**, the **Allées de la Liberté** and ...pecially on **La Croisette**. A really cos-...politan boulevard, this three kilome-...e promenade around the harbour goes ...m the **Old Port** and the **Palais des** ...ongrès (Congress Hall), built on the ...e of the old municipal casino, to the tip of **Palm-Beach**, where the modern **Casino d'Eté** and the **Port Canto** can be found. A walk along the boulevard presents quite a spectacle in itself, per-formed against a backdrop of the sea, golden beaches, swaying palms and a profusion of flowers. La Croisette has become a true symbol of the rapid expansion and new-found vocation of Cannes. The Palais de Congrès area of the boulevard concentrates together several luxury hotels –such as the *Carlton* or the *Majestic*– opulent resi-dences and fashionable name-brand boutiques. Truly this vast esplanade,

▲ *The Carlton Hotel.*

claimed from the sea and planted with pleasant gardens, is the best trump card the city holds.

Cannes extends to the north, along the Boulevard Carnot, as far as Cannet; to the west up to La Bocca along the Boulevard *Jean Hibert*, which takes in the *Plage du Midi*, and to the east, past the luxurious mansions lining the beautiful avenues of the residential areas known as *La Californie* and *Cannes-Den*.

Running parallel to La Croisette, the Rue d'Antibes is an important commer-

The Rue Meynadier.

cial centre with magnificent stores, while the Rue Meynadier displays its bustling dynamism to the world through its colourful and spirited window displays.

In the centre of the city there is **Le Suquet** hill, the ancient bulwark of Cannes where streets and houses cluster around the slopes of *Mont Chevalier*. Le Suquet has the intimate, quiet and peaceful feel of a village; in great contrast to the busy modern city beyond. The 22 metre high Suquet Tower is the building which best represents old Cannes. It was destroyed during the French Revolution, but restored on the initiative of Cannes' fishermen who had always used it as a reference point when navigating around the coast.

There is a magnificent panoramic view over Cannes available from the ancient walls of La Suquet. Overlooking the old port, Suquet is criss-crossed with charming crooked streets such as the

A street in Suquet. ▶

The old port. ▼

Cannes and the surrounding area

▲ *The Church tower of Our Lady of Hope.*

▼ *The steps up the hill of Le Suquet.*

Interior of the Our Lady of Hope Church.

▼ *La Place de la Castre.*

Rues *Mont Chevalier*, *Sant-Antoine*, *Boucherie*, *Le Pré* or *Saint-Dizier*.
Within the district can be found t
Eglise Notre-Dame de l'Espéran
(Church of Our Lady of Hope). Finish
in 1645 it is in a Southern-Gothic st
and contains altarpieces from the cla
sical era, some fine 16th century re
quary busts and from the same peri
a beautiful Virgin Mary and a remarkal
statue of Saint Anne. At the top of t
hill there is the tiny **Place de la Cast**
bordered to the north by a fragment
the 14th century ramparts. It has a w
coming aspect with shady pines and
ennobled by an interesting 16th centu
church reminiscent in structure of t
Gothic architecture. Inside the chur
many polychrome statues are to
found.

The Castre Museum, in the square, houses collections of objects as diverse as Etruscan and Hellenic sarcophagi, two lead coffins found at Sidon, a painted sarcophagus marked with the name of the scribe Imenhetep (20th Dynasty), re-Colombian pottery, Polynesian ethnography, earthenware from Asia Minor and Rhodes, Egyptian antiques, anchors, amphorae and funeral objects from the local area. The museum was founded on the collections of the rich Dutch Baron *Lycklama*. A painting of the Baron, dressed as an oriental, can be found in one of the rooms. Beyond the *alifornie* residential area of Cannes are the hills of Super-Cannes from where a splendid view of the landscape towards Estérel and the Italian border is available. The Avenue *Isola-Bella* and the ue *A.L. Sardou* lead to the observatory.

The Castre Museum.

LES ILES DE LERINS

Historically, Cannes was always closely linked to the Lerin Isles and through diverse tourist links it still is.

The tourist offer includes pleasure trips around the islands –especially frequent in summer– and a wonderfully artistic «Son et Lumière» (sound and light show).

A narrow strait called the «*Plateau Du Milieu*», which is largely frequented by private boats, separates the two islands.

▲ *Monastery on the Isle of Saint-Honorat.*

▲ *The Isle of Saint-Marguerite.*

The island of **Sainte-Marguerite**, 90 metres across and 3 kilometres long from east to west, is the larger and higher of the two. With the exception of the *Domaine du Grand Jardin*, Sainte Marguerite belongs entirely to the state. The isle is wooded with pines and eucalyptus and criss-crossed with enchanting paths. It harbours a charming little fishing village with a few shops.

The island owes its name to Saint Honorat's sister Marguerite who founded a convent here in the 5th century. Over the centuries the monastery was occupied by Visigoths, Ostrogoths and Francs, though beforehand it had been conquered by the Romans. For many centuries the island belonged to the Monks of the Lérins. However, at the beginning of the 17th century, it was ceded to the Duke of Chevreuse, later to the Duke of Guise and finally to *Jean de Bellon*. It was in this latter period that reconstruction began on the fort that currently houses the **Maritime Museum**. The **Chateau-Fort** was built by Richilieu and reinforced by Vauban. It was here that the mysterious person known to history as «*The Man in the Iron Mask*», whose identity is still a mystery, was imprisoned from 1687 to 1698. *Monsieur de Sainte-Mars*, who was in charge of the prisoner, ended up being made Governor of the Bastille in 1698 to where he took his mysterious charge who died there in 1703. The chains that bound this legendary prisoner can still be seen, as can the cell where he spent his imprisonment and the cells where the French Protestant pastors were imprisoned after the revocation of the Edict of Nantes. The Fort also served as a prison for *Maréchal Bazaine* who was there for eight months before he managed to escape in August 1874. From the terrace of the Fort there is a beautiful view of the coast with the first peaks of the Northern Alps in the background.

◀ *The Lérin Isles: St Honorat (foreground) and St Marguerite.*

e island of **Saint-Honorat**, 1,500 etres long by 400 metres across, is ry dense in pines, laurels, vines and wers. For eight centuries, from 575), the isle was the seat of the Be- dictine monks who governed Cannes d region. Today the monastery, which ffered numerous attacks throughout history, is home to some Cistercian nks. Although there are some Ro- anesque chapels on the island, the most important architectural feature is the **Castle**. Rectangular in layout, it was built as a prison fort, in the 11th centu- ry, on the site of an ancient Roman well. The Monks of the Lérins took refuge here from the attacks they were sub- jected to over the centuries. The mod- ern monastery was built in the 19th cen- tury and is surrounded by the old build- ings once occupied by the monks. The Museum has fragments of Roman and Christian engraved stones found on the isle along with documents pertaining to the monastery's history and organisa- tion. Among the seven chapels to be found on Saint-Honorat, the most in- teresting is the **Trinity Chapel** located at the eastern point of the island. In 1794, two furnaces for making cannon- balls were built here at the eastern and westernmost tips of the isle on the orders of Bonaparte.

Aerial view of La Bocca. ▼

The beaches of La Bocca. ▼

BOCCA

1834 the last few houses to the west Cannes marked where the dunes and es began; there was nothing beyond m except the Château de La Bocca d the Chapel of Saint Cassien. Then 1855 the glazier *Joseph Barthélemy* oved into the area and started off the banisation of La Bocca. Today it is an portant commercial and industrial ea with mechanics' workshops and a ipyard. Urban development in the ea has been rational and allowed for e creation of districts that are more e villages, such as *Frayère*, *Bosquet*, uéry and *Croix des Gardes*.

Cannes and the surrounding area

◀ *Aerial view.*

MANDALIEU-LA NAPOULE

This town has had many names. T Romans called it *Mantolvocus, Mand locas* or *Mandullocus*, though it did n acquire its present name until the Midc Ages. *Eucher*, the Lord of Mandalieu, generous and civilised man, liberated F slaves around the year 400 and distri uted a large part of his goods among t peasants of his fiefdom. In the 18th ce tury, Arab Pirates destroyed the tov completely. Some inhabitants refused take flight and stayed to rebuild the v lage, founding in 1706 the **Capitou**. 1782 a bridge across the Siagne w built. At the end of the 19th century, cork works was opened in near Termes that doubled the population.

▲ *The port of Rague.*

Water jets from a fountain in Mandelieu.

Mimosa, an Australian plant that was im- ported and acclimatised by the celebrat- ed horticulturist *Gilbert Nabonard*, who was from Golfe-Juan, made a significant contribution to the local economy. Mandalieu was opened out towards the sea by the building of a port at La Na- poule, some 7 kilometres from Cannes. The Lords of Villeneuve built the **Castle of Napoule**, on a rocky outcrop, in 1390. Raymond de Turenne later des- troyed it leaving only three massive square towers and their battlements. In 1919 it was rebuilt by the American Sculptor *Henry Clews* and currently houses the work of this artist. La Napoule has become a great tourist centre due to its white sands and its spa, which remains open in winter.

▼ *The Castle at La Napoule.*

General view.

HEOULE

orming a balcony that is largely open to e sea, Théoule has found a niche for elf among a chain of hills covered in eenery and flowers. Dependent on andalieu until 1929, it is now an auto- omous commune. Its four leisure ports n welcome up to 1000 boats and its eaches stretch a full 10 kilometres. ere are also some 100 kilometres of footpaths though the surrounding coun- tryside, which notably includes the Forest Park of *Eagle Point*. Theoule's offer to the holidaymaker could perhaps trump many of its more celebrated neighbours.

Not far from Théoule is the curious vil- lage of **Port la Galère**. Designed by the architect *Jacques Couelle*, the village was built on a wooded site and perfect- ly integrated into the surrounding cliffs.

The Sea Shore. ▲

Port-la-Galère. ▼

The port at Théoule.

Some views of the Cornice of L'Estérel.

MASSIF DE L'ESTEREL

Separated from the Massif des Maur⟨es⟩ by the Valley of l'Argens, the Massif ⟨de⟩ l'Estérel stretches along the Mediterr⟨a⟩nean coast from Theoule to Saint-R⟨a⟩phael. In 1903 a route along the flanks ⟨of⟩ the rocks was opened, known as t⟨he⟩ *«Corniche d'Or»* that offers some a⟨s⟩tounding views of this grandiose lan⟨d⟩scape to the visitor. The massif is form⟨ed⟩ of hard volcanic rock, largely porph⟨yry⟩ which gives the massif its remarkable f⟨iery⟩ red colour. Considerable erosion h⟨as⟩ caused the massif to take on its twist⟨ed⟩ and torn forms, creating an aggregate ⟨of⟩ impressive, sheer promontories that oft⟨en⟩ topple directly into the sea giving birth ⟨to⟩ a multitude of little islands and reefs.

From the Gulf of Napoule to Anthéor, t⟨he⟩ Massif provides an enchanting spectac⟨le⟩ with astonishing views out over to t⟨he⟩ Lerin Isles and along the coast. The su⟨m⟩mit of the massif is *Mont Vinaigre*, (Vin⟨e⟩gar Mountain) which is 618 metres high⟨.⟩

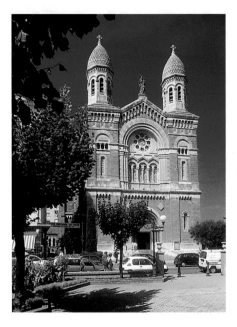

▲ The modern church in Byzantine style.

▲ The Casino.

▲ The beaches of St Raphael.

SAINT-RAPHAEL

Just opposite the town, on the last spurs to the west of l'Estérel, are the two islets of Lion de Mer and Lion de Terre which stand guard over this pretty tourist resort on the edge of the Gulf of Fréjus. Around the town are important spas such as Valescure, Boulouris, Anthéor and Trayas, which all have in common red rocks which plunge vertically into the deep blue sea.

Like Fréjus, this town has an ancient history, having once been a Roman settlement, and a Gallo-Roman village. Built on terraces and blessed with hot springs it has a plant nursery decorated with mosaics. Saracen pirates occupied and ravaged the town before being c ven out in the 10th century.

The Count of Provence ceded this te tory to the monks of the Lerins and Saint Victor of Marseilles, who creat a village here, guarded over by t Knights Templar.

On the 9th of October 1799, Bonapa came ashore here, with the future ma shals of the Empire, after returning fr his Egyptian campaign. In 1814, Nap leon passed through Saint-Rapha again accompanied by English a Austrian generals. He had been va quished and set sail from here for i prisonment on Elba.

Alphonse Karr (1808-1890) fell in lo with the town and familiarised many his artist, writer and musician frien with it.

Among the sights on offer here are t 12th century **Templar's Church**. Buil a Provencal-Romanesque style, its ap was replaced by a square watchtov that provided shelter for the townsf from pirate raids. The **Archeologi Museum** has a collection of amphor found in the Roman ruins. Although spa town, Saint-Raphael is firmly ce tred on the sea, having a fishing port yachting harbour and beaches wh are among the most beautiful on t whole coast of Var.

◄ The old port.

EJUS

ween Maures and Estérel, Frejus is ated on a rocky plateau surrounded plains covered in vines and fruit es. Caesar founded the town (as um Julii) in 49 BC on the ancient Via élia, the road from Gaul to Spain. By beginning of the Christian era, the n's port had become one of the st important in the western Mediterranean, rivalling Marseilles.

m this distant period of its past jus has preserved its arenas or phitheatres, which are the oldest in ul and were discovered in 1928. ere are also vestiges of the ancient parts and pillars and arches from its kilometre long aqueduct which car-d the water of Mons to the town.

he *Place Formigé*, in the centre of the town, there is the **Cité Episcopale** e Bishop's Seat) which is a remark-

The Place Formigé. ▲

The arenas.
Aerial view of Port-Fréjus.

able architectural ensemble. There is the Cloister, an Archaeological Museum (with a beautiful collection of Gallo-Roman antiques found at local digs) a late 4th century Baptistery, the 10th and 11th century Cathedral and the 14th century Episcopal Palace in pink, l'Estérel sandstone.

Not far from the N7 is a **Buddhist Pagoda**, built by the Vietnamese at the time of the 1914-18 war. Of note also, is the **Sudanese Mosque** within the military camp at Caïs, a reproduction of the famous Missiri of Djenné.

To the north of the town there is the

L'Estérel Safari Park, a zoo which can be visited by car and which is always popular with visitors.

Adding to the tourist attractions of the town are the various excursions available into the Massif of l'Estérel, including an interesting tour of *Mont Vinaigre* and the *Pic de l'Ours*, (Bear Peak) along with a pleasant golf course and a superb sandy beach more than 5 kilometres long.

A picturesque fountain. ▼

▲ *The port at Sainte-Maxime.*

◀ *A street inside the town.*

SAINTE-MAXIME

Sainte-Maxime lies on the northern shore of the Gulf of Saint-Tropez. It is a very pleasant site, protected and sheltered by wooded hills from the Mistral. The whole town is oriented towards its 6 kilometres of fine sandy beaches and the sea. Along the sea front, at the cen-tre of the town, on land entirely recl▮ed from the sea, the *Promenade Si▮ Lorière* offers the visitor a stroll u▮ the shade of palms and parasol pin▮ Originally a fishing port, the harbour now offer berths to 800 leisure boats. lighthouse can be visited by following pedestrian walkway that leaves from jetty whose harbour master's buildir▮ reminiscent of the prow of a ship. Facing the harbour is the old town wit▮ paved streets evoking its past. **Square Tower** dates from 1520 and built by the Monks of the Lérins. It houses a museum focused on local t▮ tions. The Parish Church has a remark▮ principal altar in serpentine coils sho▮ a permanent Provençal crib. Nearby, t▮ is the covered market where all kind▮ local produce are on display, as well as Town Hall which was formerly a silk fa▮ The Beach Casino was witness to *belle époque* when the British up▮ classes frequented the beaches Sainte-Maxime. Dating from 1928, it renovated in 1997. The *Promenade d▮ Croisette* offers a superb view of S▮ Tropez and due to its proximity to Botanical Gardens of *Myrtes*, also g▮ the stroller the possibility of resting some most relaxing natural surroundir▮

The Church towe▮

▼ *The beaches.*

RT-GRIMAUD

tly nicknamed «**The Venice of Pro-
nce**»; Port-Grimaud was built on a
mer marshland where ducks were
e hunted.

e architect *François Spoerry* con-
ved the town, which was built in the
)0s, as a place where sea, sailing
I living space could combine. His
cess can be judged by touring this
vn with its «feet in the water» in one
of the water taxis available for hire.
Here canals are streets, and boats
anchor near to houses, which are built
in a Neo-Provence style, each different
from its neighbour in aesthetic and
colour. This lacustrine town is truly
unique in its genre.

Clinging to a hill close to the town is the
old village of Grimaud with picturesque
streets and the ruins of a medieval
castle.

A street in Grimaud. ▲

The Gulf of Saint-Tropez from Port Grimaud. ▲
The roofs of Saint-Tropez. ▼

The Castle at Grimaud. ▲

SAINT-TROPEZ

Saint-Tropez lies on the southern shore
of the Gulf of the same name and is
separated from the *Bay of Cannebiers*
by a promontory. This ancient fishing
port has its own strong character and
an international reputation. Merely
evoking its name calls forth a series of
clichés of beaches, yachts and jet-set
parties full of celebrities.

Although a very fashionable resort half a
century ago, Saint-Tropez today is,
above all, a small town which has preserved its authenticity and its character.
It is an easy place to become attached
to; especially if you can take the time to
visit it calmly in the off-season.

The Var Region of the Riviera

▲ *The Old Tower district.*

Saint-Tropez appears to have been around since the dawn of recorded time. It owes its name to a centurion who, according to legend, became a Christian martyr. Decapitated on the orders of Nero, the centurion's body was placed in a small boat along with a cock and a dog. The boat drifted out to sea and where it eventually landed was built the town that bears the martyr's name.

Saint-Tropez has a rich and lively history and its inhabitants have been famed for energy and courage. Summarising the town's history, Guy de Maupassant wrote: «*This brave and briny little coastal town has fought off the Duke Anjou, the Barbery Corsairs, Constable of the Bourbons, Charles Fifth, the Duke of Savoy and the Duke Epernon. In 1637 the inhabitants, fathers of these calm bourgeoi repulsed a Spanish fleet with no exter aid. In 1813 the town also withstood English squadron sent against it*». Tod the town has to face another horde invaders, sun-seeking, friendly touri To satisfy their demands the town had to develop and has built, amo other things, a new port with immense car park. However, it has managed to jealously preserve charm and its beauty. As witness to t one only has to see the *Pétanque* pl ers in action under the shady pl trees of the *Place des Lices;* or else stroll around the streets of the old to where steep alleyways climb up hills, opening out, here and there, charming little squares, bedecked v porches and scattered with towers superb gates.

The Port is the true centre of the to It is here on the quay bearing his na that a statue was erected to commer rate the *Bailli de Sufren*. Born in 179

◀ *Tahiti-Beach.*

nt-Cannat, near Aix, *Pierre André de* *fren de Saint-Tropez*, whose family se still exists in the Place de l'Hôtel Ville was one of France's greatest men. He gained his title of *Bailli* neral) within the Order of Malta. He r served in the French Royal Navy, ing the American wars, where he ght gloriously, helping the Native ericans fight the English, before dis-earing in 1788. Following on from Quai de Suffren is the *Quai Jean* re where one can sit at the tables on terrace of the famous tea-rooms the equiér. The houses here once had ing shelters, at sea level, into which ts could directly berth.

far from the port, there is the *Musée* l'Annonciade within the ancient apel of the Annunciation. Its patron, orges Grammont transformed the apel into a museum and donated the y interesting collection of 19th and h century paintings and sculptures it sesses. There are works by Signac, ain, Marquet, Matisse, Bonnard and que, to name but a few of the artists display.

er a visit to the harbour the visitor

Partial view of the port. ▲

should now take a stroll along the *Rue de la Miséricorde* (Mercy Street), one of the most charming streets in the old town, to the **Citadel**. For four centuries this bulwark has kept watch over the turbulent town it overlooks. Construction on the building started in 1593 and finished in 1607. Since 1958 the Dungeon has housed a Naval Museum. In the main, the museum is dedicated to the history of the town and the majority of objects on display come from the Palais de Chaillot. From the Citadel there is an exceptional view of the Port, the Gulf and, in the distance, Les Maures and l'Estérel.

Built on a volcanic outcrop on the road to Ramatuelle, the 17th century **Chapelle Sainte-Anne** is a superb building containing numerous beautiful ex-votives. There is a wonderful view of Saint-Tropez and its Gulf from the church.

Near Saint-Tropez there are two superb villages **Gassin** and **Ramatuelle**, which definitely should be visited. Perched on the living rock, their crooked old streets, vaulted passageways and façades brimming with flowers are a living illustration of the indefinable charm of the old villages of Provence.

Ramatuelle. ▼

The church tower. ▲

A picturesque passageway behind ▶ *the port.*

EDITORIAL ESCUDO DE ORO, S.A.
I.S.B.N. 84-378-2168-1
Printed by FISA - Escudo de Oro, S.A.
Legal Dep. B. 32143-2005